MEXICO CITY

MARION MORRISON

WORLD ALMANAC® LIBRARY

Please visit our web site at: www.worldalmanaclibrary.com
For a free color catalog describing World Almanac® Library's list of high-quality books
and multimedia programs, call 1-800-848-2928 (USA) or 1-800-387-3178 (Canada).
World Almanac® Library's fax: (414) 332-3567.

Library of Congress Cataloging-in-Publication Data

Morrison, Marion.
    Mexico City / by Marion Morrison.
        p. cm. — (Great cities of the world)
    Includes bibliographical references and index.
    ISBN 0-8368-5023-8 (lib. bdg.)
    ISBN 0-8368-5183-8 (softcover)
    1. Mexico City (Mexico)—Juvenile literature. [1. Mexico City (Mexico).] I. Title. II. Series.
F1386.M77   2003
972'.53—dc21   2003053471

First published in 2004 by
World Almanac® Library
330 West Olive Street, Suite 100
Milwaukee, WI 53212 USA

Copyright © 2004 by World Almanac® Library.

Produced by Discovery Books
Editor: Gianna Williams
Series designers: Laurie Shock, Keith Williams
Designer and page production: Keith Williams
Photo researcher: Rachel Tisdale
Maps and diagrams: Keith Williams
World Almanac® Library editorial direction: Jenette Donovan Guntly
World Almanac® Library art direction: Tammy Gruenewald
World Almanac® Library production: Beth Meinholz

Photo credits: AKG London: p.10; AKG London/British Library: p.9; Art Directors & Trip/A. Ghazzal: p.42; Art Directors
& Trip/Ask Images: p.13; Corbis: p.5; Corbis Saba/Keith Danemiller: p.34; David Simson: p.16; Hutchison Library/Edward
Parker: p.33; Hutchison Library/Isabella Tree: cover, title page, pp.18, 19; Hutchison Library/Juliet Highet: p.21;
Hutchison Library/Liba Taylor: p.24; Hutchison Library/Sarah Murray: p.37; Panos Pictures/Mark Henley: pp.22, 27, 28,
43; Panos Pictures/Paul Smith: p.38; Panos Pictures/Piers Benatar: p.39; South American Pictures/Chris Sharp: pp.32, 35,
40; South American Pictures/Tony Morrison: pp.4, 7, 8, 12, 15, 23, 25, 26, 36; Still Pictures/Edward Parker: p.41; Still
Pictures/Julio Etchart: p.29; Still Pictures/Mark Edwards: p.20; Still Pictures/Ron Giling: p.30

Cover caption: Dancers in Mexico City celebrating the Day of Our Lady of Guadalupe.

Printed in the United States of America

1 2 3 4 5 6 7 8 9 07 06 05 04 03

Contents

Introduction

"Like a river flowing to the sea, the streets of Mexico City flow to the Zócalo, the main square, which is so beautiful it takes your breath away."

—Elena Poniatowska, Mexican writer, 2000.

Mexico City ranks just below Tokyo, Japan, as the world's largest city. At the heart of Mexico City is the Federal District, where about 8.6 million people live. From the air, you can see how two more cities and dozens of villages merge with the Federal District into one gigantic sprawl. This area, encompassing 600 square miles (1,554 square kilometers), is known as metropolitan Mexico City. It is home to

◀ *In the past fifty years, Mexico City has spread in every direction across the drying bed of Lake Texcoco.*

over eighteen million people. Mexicans refer to Mexico City simply as "DF" (for "Distrito Federal") or "Mexico."

At the Heart of the City

At the center of the city is the Great Square, which is known as the Zócalo. Officially it is called the Plaza de la Constitución and it is one of the largest squares in the world. The National Palace is located there and political demonstrations are often held in that area. In the center of the square, a huge national flag flies from sunrise to sunset and is lowered each day with a simple ceremony.

A formal park, the Alameda Central, was added in 1592 to the northeast of the square. Later, long avenues replaced much of the street grid. One well-known avenue, Insurgentes, runs 25 mi (40 km) north to south across the city. In the south, Insurgentes passes two old villages, Coyoacán and San Ángel, which are now surrounded by new development.

CITY FACTS

Mexico City
Capital of Mexico

Founded: A.D. 1325

Area: 600 sq mi (1,554 sq km)

Population (Federal District): 8,605,239 (2000)

Population (Metropolitan): 18.3 million

Population Density: 14,342 people per sq mi (5,537 per sq km)

▼ Mexico's national flag flies in the center of the Zócalo, the main square of the historic city.

Mexico City (Inset of Center)

N

miles
0   2   4
0   2   4   6
kilometers

Basilica of Guadalupe

National Museum of Anthropology

CHAPULTEPEC

Reforma

Benito Juárez International Airport

Insurgentes

SAN ÁNGEL

COYOACÁN

University City (UNAM Campus)

PEDREGAL

XOCHIMILCO

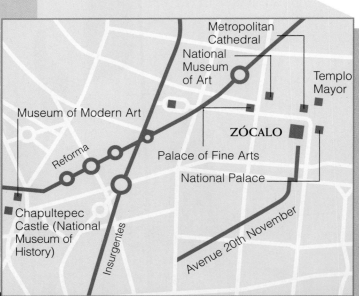

Museum of Modern Art

Reforma

Chapultepec Castle (National Museum of History)

Insurgentes

Metropolitan Cathedral

National Museum of Art

Templo Mayor

ZÓCALO

Palace of Fine Arts

National Palace

Avenue 20th November

A City Built on a Lake

Mexico City lies in the Valley of Mexico, roughly in the south-central part of the country. Low hills surround it on three sides, but to the southeast stand two magnificent snow-covered volcanoes. On a clear day, they are visible from the city center. On the right is Popocatépetl, or "smoking mountain," and on the left is Iztaccíhuatl, or "white lady."

"Glimpsed in the early morning from between pine branches where the road swings over the pass, Mexico City lies a thousand feet below, webbed in a light haze but with glass towers glinting under a brilliant sky…"

—John Lincoln, writer, 1963.

▲ The Metropolitan Cathedral is sinking. Engineers extracted soft clay through drill holes to level the building and braced the interior with scaffolding.

The Valley of Mexico was once covered by five lakes. In the fourteenth century, the Aztec people built their capital, Tenochtitlán, on an island in the largest lake, Texcoco. Later, Spanish invaders built Mexico City on top of Tenochtitlán and drained the lake to expand their city.

Seasons at High Altitude

At 7,350 feet (2,240 meters) above sea level, the days are often warm and the nights cool. In the wet season, from May to September or even earlier, sudden storms with rain, thunder, and lightning sometimes fill the sky. Streets run with torrents of water and rain washes away some of the air pollution from which Mexico City suffers so badly. In summer, it can be warm—with a high of 90 °F (32 °C)—but the winters are cooler, often about 50 °F (10 °C), and snow falls on the surrounding volcanoes.

A Sinking City

Mexico City has been sinking for a long time. Many of Mexico City's historic monuments are now standing many feet below their original level.

By the 1980s, it was feared the massive Metropolitan Cathedral would collapse. Visitors now enter through the main entrance to the cathedral by a slope leading downhill for about 7 ft (2 m). Urgent action was required to save the building. Engineers had to support the interior of the cathedral with a web of scaffolding. Sodden clay from the lake bed was taken out through boreholes. A little was taken here and a little there until the building slowly leveled. As the situation has improved, most of the scaffolding has been removed.

CHAPTER 1

History of Mexico City

M exico City is the oldest continuously inhabited city in the Americas. Sometime in the early twelfth century, Native American Aztecs (also known as Mexica) left their homeland, probably in the north of Mexico. They wandered for over a century. According to legend, the spot where they were to settle would be revealed by their god, Huitzilopochtli. The sign they looked for was an eagle perched on a nopal cactus eating a serpent. The Aztecs eventually arrived in the Valley of Mexico in A.D. 1325, where they saw the sign and founded Tenochtitlán.

Templo Mayor

In 1978, some men working for a power company were digging close to the Metropolitan Cathedral. About 7 ft (2 m) underground, they found a massive, almost perfectly circular stone (left). The surface was carved with designs believed to represent Coyolxauhqui, the sister of Huitzilopochtli. Over the next four years, archaeologists uncovered the remains of Tenochtitlán's Templo Mayor, or "Great Temple." The temple was a pyramid with seven layers. At the base were eight life-sized stone sculptures of unidentified human figures.

Tenochtitlán and Tlatelolco

Tenochtitlán began as a collection of homes made of reeds surrounding the temple of Huitzilopochtli. About a mile to the north, another tribe had settled on a similar island known as Tlatelolco, or "the place of the mounds." The twin settlements developed and were connected by causeways. One Spanish invader observed the causeways were wide enough "to allow ten horsemen to ride abreast." There was plenty of food for the people of Tenochtitlán to eat. Water was carried by an aqueduct from a spring on Chapultepec Hill. They grew crops of maize, chili peppers, squash, and tomatoes on fields known as *chinampas*, little islands that they had built above the level of the water.

Tenochtitlán was ruled by chiefs until its first king was installed in 1376. Stone buildings replaced the simple reed

▲ *This seventeenth-century illustration shows Lake Texcoco with causeways, the island, and temples.*

"We turned to look at the great plaza and the multitude of people there, some buying and others selling, and just the murmur and hum of the voices and the words spoken resounded for more than a league and among us were soldiers who had been in many parts of the world… and they said they had never seen a plaza so large, so busy, and with so many people."

—Bernal Diaz del Castillo, sixteenth-century chronicler.

dwellings. Grand temples and palaces were built. Gradually, the Aztecs grew more powerful and conquered many neighboring tribes. In 1473, they seized nearby Tlatelolco. Within about 150 years of the founding of Tenochtitlán, the Aztec Empire covered much of modern-day Mexico. By the time the Spaniards arrived in 1519, Tenochtitlán and Tlatelolco had more than 200,000 inhabitants. That was more than in any European city at the time.

Spanish Rule

When Spanish conqueror Hernán Cortés landed on the coast of what is now Mexico in March 1519, he was well prepared. He led 530 men with horses, cannon, and small arms. Two earlier expeditions had given reports of a hostile welcome by the people of the Yucatán in the southeast of Mexico. On one occasion, some Spaniards had been sacrificed and eaten. Cortés encountered some opposition, but as he ventured westward, he began to make friends and in one town he was given a young girl, Malinche, as an interpreter.

The Aztecs believed that the Spaniards were gods returning to their homeland. At first, the Aztec emperor, Moctezuma (sometimes known as Montezuma), treated them kindly, but the Spaniards exploited differences and forged alliances with neighboring groups hostile to the Aztecs.

Shadows of the Aztec Past

In addition to the Great Temple of Tenochtitlán, there are other reminders of Aztec civilization in Mexico City. In the north, ancient pyramids, such as the serpent pyramid of Tenayuca and the temple pyramid at Santa Cecilia Acatitlán, still stand. And, people continue to grow fruit and vegetables on the Aztec chinampas.

▶ *A depiction of the destruction of Tenochtitlán by Spanish invaders.*

The first Spanish attempt to take Tenochtitlán failed. Cortés took Moctezuma hostage and tried to force him to subdue his people. By some accounts, Moctezuma was stoned to death by Aztecs angry at the ruler's apparent betrayal.

The Spaniards first laid siege to Tenochtitlán in 1520. They built ships to cross the lake, and attacked with the help of at least 50,000 Native allies. On August 13, 1521, at the end of another siege, the last Aztec king, Cuauhtémoc, was captured near Tlatelolco, signaling the Aztecs' surrender.

Historians believe that around 100 Spaniards died during the last siege. However, about 100,000 Aztecs and other Native peoples died during that battle and later from smallpox and other diseases unwittingly introduced by the Spaniards.

The Spanish adventurers destroyed much of the city, including Aztec temples, which they replaced with simple churches. Soon after, Catholic priests arrived from Spain and began to convert the Native Americans to Christianity.

A European City

Within 75 years of the Spanish conquest, over 15,000 Spanish residents lived in the city, though some accounts quote as many as 40,000. Native Americans and *mestizos* (people of mixed Spanish and Native American descent) accounted for about 80,000. There were also about 50,000 Africans brought by the Spanish as slaves.

As the population became more European, so did the city. In 1607, as the need for more land grew, work began to drain Lake Texcoco to create space.

"The gallants [smart gentlemen] of this city shew [show] themselves daily, some on horseback, and most in coaches, about four of the clock in the afternoon in a pleasantly shady field called la Alameda, full of trees and walks."

—Thomas Gage, missionary, early seventeenth century.

Plaza de las Tres Culturas

Mexico City has preserved signs of its turbulent history everywhere. In one square, the Plaza de las Tres Culturas (Square of the Three Cultures), three civilizations are represented: Aztec, Spanish, and modern Mexican cultures. The square was the former site of the great Tlatelolco market, the center of trade for the Aztec empire. The Spanish conquerors were astounded by its size, as it rivaled or surpassed European markets.

An Aztec pyramid with two staircases has also been uncovered on this site. On one side of the plaza stands the Spanish Templo de Santiago, first built in 1524 and then rebuilt in 1609. On another side of the plaza is the modern twentieth-century glass and concrete building of the Secretariat of Foreign Relations.

The Fight for Freedom

The Spaniards governed Mexico for almost three hundred years, but the Mexicans came to hate the rules and taxes imposed by Spain. By the early 1800s, the situation had reached the boiling point. The people successfully fought for their independence, and Mexico became a republic in 1821.

The newly independent country experienced a period of great turmoil. There were fifty governments between 1821 and 1871. Mexico at independence included the vast areas of present-day Texas, California, and the entire American southwest.

In 1846, Mexico went to war over the annexation of Texas and claims on California by the United States. In 1847, the United States invaded and seized Mexico City, forcing the Mexican government to give up what is now Texas, New Mexico, and California in return for the city's release and the sum of $15 million.

Benito Juárez

In 1855, a new liberal government began to reduce the influence of the Catholic Church. The government closed churches, convents, and missions, and many were turned into offices or schools. This angered the wealthy families of Spanish descent. In 1857, a civil war began, which the liberal government's supporters won in 1861. Benito Juárez, a Zapotec Native American, then became president.

An Imperial City

Because of the new nation's inability to pay its debts, British, Spanish, and French armies landed on the shores of Mexico.

▼ *Benito Juárez was president of Mexico from 1861 to 1862 and from 1867 to 1872.*

After reaching a settlement, Britain and Spain withdrew, but the French remained and took Mexico City. Austrian Archduke Maximilian was brought in to govern. In 1867, amid Mexican resistance, Maximilian surrendered and was executed.

A New President and New Investment

In 1876, Porfirio Díaz became president. A stern dictator, he nevertheless attracted investments to the new country and developed Mexico City. Railroads and mines were constructed throughout the country and a drainage canal system was built to end flooding in Mexico City. In the late nineteenth century, dozens of grand mansions were built along the Paseo de la Reforma (usually shortened to just the Reforma). New districts were created, known as delegaciones and colonias. By the beginning of the twentieth century, the population had reached almost 400,000.

Chapultepec Castle

Emperor Maximilian lived in a castle on Chapultepec Hill (below), connected to Alameda Central by a dirt road. In 1864, he decided that the road should be made into a grand, tree-lined avenue called the Paseo del Emperador—the Emperor's Parade. After his death, the Emperor's Parade was changed to the Paseo de la Reforma. In 1937, Chapultepec Hill became a national monument. Two floors of the castle are taken up by the National Museum of History. To reach the castle, visitors have to walk from the park gate, but it is worth the effort to see the spectacular view of the city from the hill.

Under Porfirio Díaz, many houses were built on the land between the old city center and the Paseo de la Reforma. One of the most fascinating architectural areas is Colonia Roma, where many wealthy people bought land and built European-style homes. Most ordinary people of that time lived in simple one-story adobe buildings with flat roofs and few, if any, windows.

Another Revolution

By 1910, the Mexicans had had enough of Porfirio Díaz. After more than thirty years in power, he faced mounting opposition led by Francisco Madero. Díaz threw Madero into jail, but then allowed him to leave the country. In November 1910, from the safety of Texas, Madero, backed by revolutionaries Emiliano Zapata and Francisco "Pancho" Villa, called for rebellion. Within six

1968 Olympic Games

In 1968, Mexico City hosted the Olympic Games. The regente *(mayor) cleaned up the city, built new roads, and started the metro, or subway system. The Olympic flame arrived in Mexico City on September 12. Aware the world's press was focused on the games, Mexican students protested in the Plaza de las Tres Culturas against working conditions and a lack of jobs. Tragically, city authorities met them with force. On October 2, the police and soldiers opened fire. Between 150 and 300 students died.*

months, the revolution succeeded and Díaz fled to Europe. Madero was elected president. He faced many problems before being captured and assassinated by his opponents in 1913. More turmoil followed until a relatively peaceful period following the adoption of a new constitution in 1917.

Beginning in the 1920s, large numbers of people migrated from the countryside to Mexico City. In 1921, the population reached 900,000; by 1940, it had almost doubled, and, by the 1950s, it hit 3 million.

The PRI

In the second half of the twentieth century, Mexico City grew and so did social divisions. A student rebellion in 1968 struck against the social system, but the movement died amid violent suppression and a lack of support by PRI-controlled union workers. By 1977, half of all workers received only 13.5 percent of the country's income, causing great dissatisfaction.

The Partido Revolucionario Institucional (PRI) grew from the National Revolutionary Party, first founded in 1929, and remained elected in power until 2000, the world's longest political run. The movement against the party gained momentum, however, during the 1980s. By the elections of 1994, tens of thousands of demonstrators were gathering in the Zócalo to protest. In the elections of 2000, the party lost and Vicente Fox Quesada of PAN—the National Action Party—assumed the presidency.

◄ The Latin American Tower skyscraper, built in 1956, resembles New York's Empire State Building. It has forty-four floors and for many years was Mexico's tallest building. From the 42nd floor, the view across the city is spectacular. On a clear day, the view includes the surrounding mountains and snow-capped volcanoes.

CHAPTER 2

People of Mexico City

It is only in the last fifty years that Mexico City's population has grown so large. At the beginning of the 1950s, the population was less than New York, Paris, or London at that time. By 1970, it had reached 9.1 million and experts were sure it would double in twenty years. It rose to 13.9 million by 1980, about 15.6 million by 1995, and, though slowing, it now looks set to crash through the 20 million barrier sometime before 2015.

Most of today's inhabitants of Mexico City are mestizos. There are very few descendants of the original Spanish conquerors, and immigrants from Europe are a minority. The numbers of African Mexicans, pure Native Americans, and Asian immigrants are small.

In some areas of Mexico City, such as Polanco, San Ángel, and Pedregal de San Ángel, though, the population is almost entirely mestizo, and the people have a noticeably more European appearance. These are affluent suburbs and residential areas where many immigrants have settled. Occasionally, people of Jewish descent are seen, in orthodox dress, in Polanco. The so-called "Barrio Chino," or Chinese quarter, is

◄ *A young girl sells candles to worshipers outside the Metropolitan Cathedral in the Zócalo.*

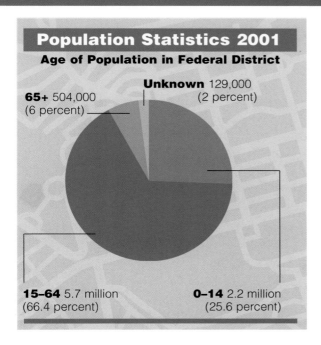

Population Statistics 2001
Age of Population in Federal District

65+ 504,000
(6 percent)

Unknown 129,000
(2 percent)

15–64 5.7 million
(66.4 percent)

0–14 2.2 million
(25.6 percent)

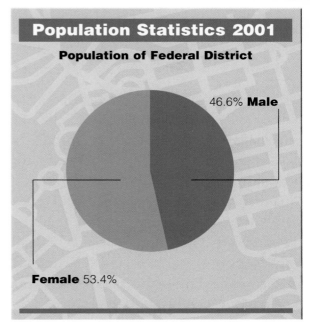

Population Statistics 2001
Population of Federal District

46.6% **Male**

Female 53.4%

▲ *The population of Mexico City is relatively youthful. More than a quarter of residents are under the age of fourteen. There also are more females than males.*

remembered by a clock known as the "Chinese Clock." Other signs have all but disappeared of the Chinese community that once lived there.

Language of the Aztecs

The language of the Aztecs, Náhuatl, has survived in many of the place names in Mexico. Náhuatl names are not as difficult to pronounce as they look. The x has the sound of the English sh; z is like the English s; and hu, when it is before a vowel, is said like a w. The vowels in Mexican names are pronounced as they would be in modern Spanish. "Náhuatl" is pronounced "Naw-wa-tul," and "Nezahualcóyotl" is pronounced "Nets-a-wahl-CO-yotl."

In recent years, more people have been arriving from South Korea to work in new industries. Approximately one hundred Korean companies have invested in Mexico since 1995. Mexico has thirty-two trade agreements with other countries and regions. Because of its proximity to the United States, Mexico is also seen as the gateway to Latin America. While one third of all industries in Mexico are based in Mexico City, there are several large industries in other areas: textiles in Puebla, skins and shoe making in Guanajuato, and the multinational companies Samsung (electronics) and L.G. Korea Ltd. (which makes car batteries) located in Tijuana.

Religion in Mexico City

Although the vast majority of the population of Mexico City is Catholic, nowadays most people only rarely attend one of the many churches in the city. On the other hand, the average Mexican

On the other hand, the average Mexican will almost certainly have made the pilgrimage to the sacred Shrine of Guadalupe on the hill of Tepeyac to the north of the city.

Other faiths are represented in Mexico City, but these belong to the minority foreign-born population. There is at least one Jewish synagogue and a Buddhist center, while Protestant Evangelists work mostly via the radio and Internet.

Churches of Mexico City

When the Spanish colonists built the city, they wanted a major church to match the cathedral in Seville, Spain. Thus, they built the massive Metropolitan Cathedral in the Zócalo. Begun in the late sixteenth century, it was completed in 1813. It has fourteen side chapels, five naves, and sixteen massive columns to support the roof. Inside the front doors is the Altar del Perdón, where prisoners condemned by the Inquisition had to "face God" before being executed.

Apart from the cathedral, the most important churches are the old and new Basilicas of Guadalupe. The old basilica (completed in 1709) is now too small for large crowds. The new basilica, built in 1976, is extraordinary and controversial. Made of concrete, it can hold over 20,000 people.

There are many other churches in the city, often with ornate, carved façades and gold-leaf altars. One historic example is the

▲ Dancers celebrate the festival of the Virgin in front of the new Basilica of Guadalupe.

Church of San Francisco, once part of a Franciscan monastery founded by Hernán Cortés in 1524. The church is now sinking.

Festivals

The principal religious festival for the people of Mexico City and for most Mexicans is the Holy Day of the Virgin of Guadalupe, the country's patron saint. Every year on the days leading up to December 12, thousands of pilgrims visit the Shrine of Guadalupe, comprising several old chapels

Piñatas

One popular Mexican custom at Christmas is to break a piñata. Piñatas are earthenware pots filled with candy. The pots are covered with colored foil and made into the shape of a cone, star, or Santa Claus. On Christmas Eve, piñatas are hung in a room or over a street, where blindfolded children try to smash them with sticks. When the pot bursts, all the candy is scattered and the children scramble to pick up as much as they can hold.

"In Mexico, where the legacy of Aztec rule has become intertwined with four centuries of Catholicism, the Dia de los Muertos or Day of the Dead is a unique celebration of death, of the cycle of life, and the personality and spirituality of the people."

—Octavio Paz, Mexican poet, 1997.

and the old and new basilicas, built to cope with the increasingly large number of pilgrims. Many pilgrims make the last part of the journey on their knees. The main avenue to the shrine is lined with stalls filled with all kinds of religious mementos and tables where families can sit and eat. The festival-goers celebrate with pageants, dancing, and singing, and some people wear richly colored Aztec costumes. Others wear costumes from their specific regions.

The Day of the Dead, which is actually a two-day festival in November, is celebrated by most Mexican families. People visit cemeteries and take flowers to the graves of dead friends and relatives. Special altars are made in their honor, with gifts of their favorite foods or other items. Special foods include little skulls and skeletons made of sugar and chocolate. Market sellers often construct altars in their stalls, where they display their Day of the Dead bread, offerings, and photos of ancestors.

▶ *Skeletons and skulls made of chocolate, sugar, and bread are sold for the Day of the Dead celebration.*

19

World-Famous Cuisine

Mexican food is famous all over the world. The main ingredients are chili peppers, corn, chocolate, and squash. Dozens of delicious Mexican recipes combine the flavors of spices and meat with vegetables such as beans, avocado, and tomato. Corn *tortillas*, flat cornmeal cakes, are filled with meat and seasonings before being rolled, folded, sometimes fried, or toasted. Often, they are sprinkled with soft white cheese. Refried beans are also found everywhere.

A recipe typical of the Valley of Mexico is *chicharrones*, dried pork rinds, in different sauces. *Tamales*, corn meal filled with meat and wrapped in corn husks, are a favorite everywhere. A local variety of tamale is

▲ *Mexican cooking starts with fresh produce, like the vegetables sold loose at these market stalls.*

filled with young *nopales* (cactus), chopped onion, and a green herb called *epazote*. This herb is an ingredient in many Mexican dishes and was once used as a medicine.

It was the Aztecs that introduced the world to chocolate. *Cacao* (chocolate) beans from the warmer lands below the mountains were used by the Aztecs as money and chocolate drinks were often made for special occasions.

One traditional Mexican food that includes chocolate is *mole poblano*. It comes from Puebla, a city south of the capital. The mole, or sauce, includes five different types unsweetened chocolate. Mole is served most often with chicken, tortillas, and refried beans.

Stalls and Cafés

Hardly a street in Mexico City is without a food stall. Mexicans often stop and snack as they go about their work. Restaurants, on the other hand, are meeting places for people who can afford their prices.

The Café Tacuba, near the city center, was founded at the time of the revolution. Known for its food and desserts, a mural showing the uses of chocolate decorates one wall of the café. The café is so famous, a Mexican rock band has taken its name.

The House of Tiles

The extraordinary House of Tiles dates back to the 1500s and was the home of the Count of Valle de Orizaba. The outside walls are decorated with painted tiles from Puebla, a district to the southeast of Mexico City. The house has had several owners during its long history. In 1919, it was converted into a restaurant and coffee shop by Walter and Frank Sanborn, two Americans who arrived in the capital in 1903 and began a business founded largely on ice cream. Sanborn's ice cream is still sold in the House of Tiles.

▼ Tortillas are made by cooking flattened cornmeal dough on a hot steel griddle.

CHAPTER 3

Living in Mexico City

Living in Mexico City is a challenge for almost everyone. The majority of Mexicans' homes are simple, usually a house or an apartment of just two or three small rooms and a bedroom.

Tlatelolco Housing Project

As Mexico City began to grow rapidly, the government realized that providing housing for everybody would be a problem. Architects decided to create enormous buildings designed for a compact lifestyle. Families could live in apartments of three or four rooms within a building and share the parking space below. Stores, banks, schools, and recreation centers were included. One of the most ambitious plans, developed between 1962 and 1964, was for apartments in Tlatelolco, 4 mi (6.5 km) north of the Zócalo. Ten thousand apartments were created with easy access to the city center. The huge complex is still there, although it was damaged in an earthquake in 1985.

A Typical Family

The Morales family is a typical Mexican family. They live in a house they are still building located about 6 mi (9.5 km) from

◄ *Apartment buildings are crowded together in the far east of the city just south of Nezahualcóyotl.*

Earthquakes

Earthquakes or earth tremors happen often in Mexico City. Earth tremors are magnified as they pass through the old lake bed and sometimes the result has been devastating. Early on September 19, 1985, the city was struck by an earthquake of 8.1 on the Richter scale. The official death toll was 10,000, but unofficial figures were as high as 30,000 dead and 50,000 injured. The destroyed building in this picture (left) was a car park.

the Zócalo. The house has a small yard, two rooms downstairs, and three tiny bedrooms on the second floor. The Moraleses have a small television and cook on a small stove using bottled gas to make typical meals such as rice, beans, chicken, and tortillas. Their large dog, Loco, serves as a guard dog, protecting their house from crime, which is common in their neighborhood.

"Neza" and the Lost Cities

Vast urban areas where many poor people live have become cities in their own right. The largest is Nezahualcóyotl. About two million people live in "Neza." Like the Federal District, Neza has become a magnet for people from the countryside who want a better life. It is a thrown-together mass of unfinished roads, low-cost housing, shanty homes, and garbage heaps. It is Mexico's third largest city, but is considered part of metropolitan Mexico City. Neza is the extreme of poverty. Many inhabitants find work sorting the city's trash.

Then there are the *ciudades perdidas*, or lost cities, which spring up overnight as more country people arrive with their worldly goods in sacks or boxes. These places are without water, and electricity is usually pirated from the nearest pole. The dwellings range from simple structures built from the best trash available—wood, beaten-out tin cans, plastic, and so on—to houses made from concrete blocks, with windows and doors. Like all unplanned shantytowns, they grow and develop without planning permission, eventually becoming part of the city.

At the other extreme are the tall apartment buildings of Polanco or Pedregal de San Ángel, or the fine houses of the

Lomas de Chapultepec, concealed behind high walls and hedges and watched over by security guards.

Shopping in Mexico City

Shopping in Mexico City can be exciting. At one time, the Zona Rosa area south of the Reforma was famous for elegant shops, but now there are similar shops in other places with less congestion and pollution. If people want a shiny new Lamborghini or Ferrari, there is a glitzy showroom in Polanco. For huge selections of handicrafts

▼ *Colorful weavings, clothes, and beaded jewelry made by Native American craftspeople are sold at weekend tourist markets.*

from all over the country, shoppers go to the Buena Vista market. The size of a soccer field, it is packed with colorful goods. For charms and Native American medicines, people head for the narrow, dark passages of the Sonora, or "Witches' Market."

Food Markets

There are a great many food markets and some are enormous. In simple public markets, meat and fish are sold loose (packaged foods are rare except in a few shops in wealthier districts). Eggs are sold on cardboard trays, not in egg cartons; fruit is piled high; and there is an amazing array of baskets filled with peppers. Herbs are sold from sacks.

Nacional Monte de Piedad

One of the city's great institutions is the main office of the Nacional Monte de Piedad, the national pawnshop. Anyone who needs to borrow money can take an item of value—a ring, watch, or painting—and leave it at the pawnshop in return for part of its value. Later, when the money (plus interest) is paid back, the item is returned to its owner. Some goods are never bought back by their original owners and the pawnshop is a treasure house of watches, clocks, jewelry, porcelain, and art for sale to everyone. The Monte de Piedad stands on the site of the Axayatl Palace of Moctezuma.

Department Stores

For a city of eighteen million people, department stores are surprisingly rare. Two of the most famous stand opposite each other on the Avenue 20th of November, which leads south from the Zócalo. The Palacio de Hierro, or Iron Palace, was built at the end of the nineteenth century. Today, the palace is the flagship store for a chain of seven, selling high-priced, quality goods. Its window displays equal those of any major city. Across the street, another store, the Liverpool, has a 1920s Art Deco front.

▶ *Just a few steps from the Zócalo, the nineteenth-century Palacio de Hierro, or Iron Palace, department store is one of the city's landmarks.*

Education in Mexico City

Education is compulsory and free between the ages of six and fifteen in Mexico, but about 15 percent of eligible children do not attend. These are mostly children from poorer families who must work at a young age. As the city is growing so fast, new schools are being built all the time. Most schools are run by the government; others are run by the church; and there are also private schools. Children study sciences, languages, arts, history, and geography. Physical education is a popular subject.

Primary school lasts six years and is divided into two levels, basic and higher, each taking three years. High school has a three-year curriculum, with an additional three years for students intending to go to college. Students at public schools have to wear a uniform. Girls have gray, pleated skirts and blue blouses, while boys wear blue pants and a white shirt. Some wear track suits in their school's colors.

Sessions

Because there are so many students, the school day is divided into morning and afternoon sessions. In high school, the session a student attends depends on grades. Those with good grades usually attend morning sessions. Grades run from a failing grade of 5, to 10 (excellent), but are broken down by decimals, such as 7.3, 8.9, etc. A good student needs to get an 8 and above in all subjects to remain in morning sessions.

Proof of Mexico City's success in education is the literacy rate, which is high compared to the national average: about 96.7 percent of the city's population over fifteen can read and write.

Private Education

Private schools are usually found in areas close to the wealthier residential districts. These schools are less crowded than public schools, but the work is similar. Private schools include the American School, the Alexander von Humboldt German College, and a Mexican-British school. There are also private institutions for art and science, and colleges and universities.

◄ *Education in Mexico City is an important part of daily life. Classes in private schools like this one are smaller than those in enormous state institutions.*

▲ *UNAM students pose for photographs on graduation day.*

Colleges

From high school, some students go on to college. The city is famous for its National Autonomous University of Mexico, also known as UNAM. It is one of the largest universities in the world with over 300,000 students. Founded in 1551, it is now located on a magnificent campus, University City, near the old villages of Coyoacán and San Ángel. The outside walls of some of the buildings are covered with huge drawings or murals made of colored tiles. A hotbed of student politics in the 1960s, it boasts a ten-story, internationally famous library building decorated with a mosaic mural by Juan O'Gorman. He was an artist during the muralist movement, which left such an indelible mark on Mexico City's cultural history.

Another exceptional institution is the Autonomous University of Chapingo, to the east of the Benito Juárez International Airport. The university's chapel is a national treasure filled with murals by famous Mexican artist Diego Rivera.

Other universities in Mexico City include the Universidad Autónoma Metropolitana (Metropolitan Autonomous University), the Colegio de México, and the Instituto Politécnico Nacional.

Those students who do not go to college have the option of attending language schools or technical schools. However, many thousands of young people go straight from high school to work.

Living with Pollution

The furious pace of Mexico City's growth has had a seriously negative impact on its environment. Past policies favored making Mexico City the heart of the country's industrial production, but at a level that the natural environment could not sustain.

As a result, Mexico City is one of the most polluted cities in the world. The air contains almost twice the weight of particles (tiny solid pieces of pollutants) recommended by the World Health Organization. This terrible problem is caused by the city's three million automobiles, its industry, and its millions of residents. Because the city is in a valley, the wind cannot blow away pollution.

The view of the city from the top of the Latin American Tower is sometimes so bad that even the hill of Tepeyac, with the yellow-domed roof of the old Basilica of Guadalupe, is lost in a yellow haze.

Sometimes early in the mornings, before the air has been warmed by the sun, a dense band of polluted air lays across the city like a blanket. Then, suddenly, the conditions can change and the haze lifts. It may vanish altogether and, for a few hours or sometimes days, the mountains surrounding the valley will appear as sharp as a blade.

Taking Steps

By the 1980s, pollution had become so serious that the government began to limit the number of automobiles allowed in the city. It banned certain license plate numbers on different days. The ban is still in place, and the numbers are shown in the newspapers and on the Internet. On a particularly bad day, the city government may ban two sets of license plate numbers.

▼ *Traffic gridlock in the Mexico City rush hour. Car fumes are contributing to the high levels of pollution.*

▲ *As Mexico City sits in a basin, there is often not enough wind to blow pollution away.*

Each day, an air quality index is published for the city, with lists of various harmful gases present. When it reaches the danger level, schools and factories are closed.

In September 2002, 350,000 cars were banned for a day from the city as ozone levels reached 240. On th ozone scale, 100 is considered the acceptable level and 200 is considered dangerous. Ground-level ozone is a pollutant created when sunlight reacts with car and factory emissions.

Sometimes forest fires around Mexico City make an already bad pollution problem much worse. In 1998, an extreme drought caused forest fires to burn out of control in the southern Mexican states of Oaxaca and Chiapas, raising the ozone level to 251. Forty percent of the 3.5 million cars in the city were banned, schools were closed, and factories were shut, as were 20 percent of the city's gas stations.

Clean Water

Air pollution is just one of many problems. Keeping Mexico City supplied with fresh water is another challenge. For many years, water has been pumped from wells drilled into the old bed of Lake Texcoco, beneath the city, making it sink even more. Between 1940 and 1985, the ground in the downtown area of the city sank by more than 23 ft (7 m). Boreholes for water now go much deeper and the sinking has slowed, but there is still a water shortage. Today, some water is brought to the city from rivers outside the valley—an expensive process.

Getting rid of waste is another problem. As the city started to sink, drains that flowed gently downhill began to tilt upward instead. Expensive pumping was required to keep sewage flowing through one of the main drainage canals. The solution was to build a tunnel at a 100-ft (30-m) incline deep below the city. Sewage and water waste now leave the valley through this deep drainage system.

29

CHAPTER 4

Mexico City at Work

The Reforma is lined with the glass office buildings of banks and financial institutions. Well-dressed business people drive in to work and frequent the clubs and restaurants nearby. This is not the life of the average employee in Mexico City, however.

Industry

A large percentage of urban workers are employed in industry and in jobs providing services to other residents and tourists. More than a third of Mexico's industry is located in Mexico City, where factories produce chemicals, plastics, cement, and textiles. In the 1980s, there was growing concern about pollution. Industry and businesses were encouraged to move away from the capital into other regions. It worked to some extent, but Mexico City is still the industrial heart of the country.

People who work in Mexico City are slightly better off than in other parts of the country. While the national minimum wage is 39.74 pesos ($4.24) per day, the minimum wage in Mexico City is 42.15 pesos ($4.50) per day.

◀ *This boy is making a living for himself by carving wooden animal figures.*

Street Work

Many people earn a living by selling on the streets. Around the tourist centers, stalls sell posters, old photos dating from the time of the revolution, or just simple souvenirs. Streets on the west side of the Zócalo are packed with sellers. Pirated CDs are piled on plastic sheets that can be gathered up quickly when the police approach. Tourists and Mexicans alike jostle in the crowd, hunting for bargains.

In some parts of the city, young children wash car windows for a few cents at traffic-light intersections. On the streets, people try to sell phone cards, newspapers, and flowers. People make a living by collecting trash. Known as *pepenadores*—a local word meaning one who picks up or sifts through something—they are paid by bosses who then sell the results of the scavenging. It is a very profitable business, but only for the wealthy people at the top.

Waiting for Work

One of the traditions of the Zócalo is its use as a market for work. Men gather daily in front of the wrought iron railings of the Metropolitan Cathedral to offer their services—as plumbers or painters, for example. They advertise their trade on large cards alongside their piles of tools. While waiting for customers, they stand and chat with each other. Men who write and type letters or documents for a fee stand under the columns of Santo Domingo Square.

Unemployment is high—out of a total population of 8.6 million people, only 3.7 million have jobs—and with it has come more crime. Muggings and theft are common, even in broad daylight. Crime has been driving tourists away from the capital. To combat this, more "tourist police" have been drafted into the city center.

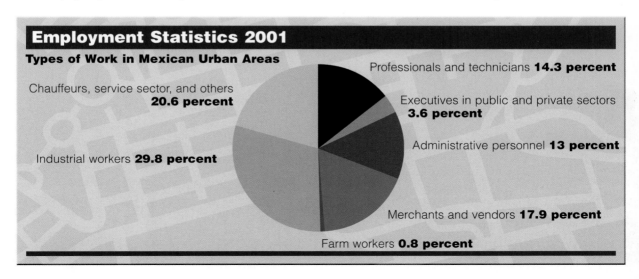

Employment Statistics 2001

Types of Work in Mexican Urban Areas

Chauffeurs, service sector, and others **20.6 percent**

Industrial workers **29.8 percent**

Professionals and technicians **14.3 percent**

Executives in public and private sectors **3.6 percent**

Administrative personnel **13 percent**

Merchants and vendors **17.9 percent**

Farm workers **0.8 percent**

Getting Around Mexico City

In such a densely populated city, traffic management is a priority. To ease the flow of traffic, some major routes, known as *ejes*, were constructed above existing roads and were lined with protective barriers. A major route, the "peripheral ring," was built around much of the city. Nezahualcóyotl and the industrial area of Tlalnepantla are linked by fast routes and the traffic moves smoothly except at rush hour. At some intersections, police officers guide the traffic.

There are several other options for commuters who cannot drive to work. Some use buses or the smaller micro-buses, called *peseros*. Others use taxis. Many of the taxis are Volkswagen "Beetles" painted a bright green or yellow. Street names in Mexico City can be confusing as sometimes there will be several streets with the same name, but in different parts of the city. Cab drivers often talk from car to car, asking other drivers the way.

A New Airport

Benito Juárez International Airport, east of the city, was at one time surrounded by open land, but the spectacular growth of Nezahualcóyotl has engulfed it. A new airport is needed, though the location is a subject for heated debate. One proposal was to build it on the old, flat lake bed of Lake Texcoco, well to the east of the city, but farmers have protested that it will take up their land, so the idea has been dropped.

The Metro

Though considered a subway system, much of Mexico City's metro is actually above ground and some is even elevated above the streets. One of the largest in the world, the metro has eleven lines with a total of more than 126 mi (200 km) of track.

▼ *Numerous brightly colored Volkswagen "Beetle" taxis sweep around the Zócalo during much of the day.*

The metro first opened in 1969 with just sixteen stations. The system grew quickly, although planners had to consider the problems of digging into the old lake bed. Many relics from Aztec times were uncovered by the tunnelers and they even found a small pyramid. Remains of a woolly mammoth were found when the foundations were dug for Talismán Station in the north.

▲ *The metro in Mexico City is clean, efficient, and largely above ground.*

The metro expanded rapidly in the 1980s to keep pace with the growing city. Today, four million people use the metro on a daily basis. The system plays an essential role in keeping down the levels of traffic and pollution, and is a cheap, reliable source of transportation for commuters.

Governing Mexico City

Governing Mexico City is not an easy job. For many years, the top post was held by a *regente* appointed by the ruling national political party. That changed during the 1990s. As part of electoral reforms that were introduced in 1996, Mexico City was given its own law-making powers and its own civil and penal code. In 1997, Mexico City elections were held for the Legislative Assembly, the city's council. That same year, inhabitants of Mexico City were given their first opportunity to elect their own mayor directly. Cuauhtémoc Cárdenas of the Partida de la Revolución Democrática (PRD) party won with 48 percent of the vote. The mayor now keeps an eye on the running of all departments from garbage disposal to the police.

While the elected mayor has overall responsibility for the city council, each of the sixteen *delegaciones*, or districts of the city, has its own leader and officers to help local people. In 2000, a new mayor and new heads of the delegaciones were elected for six years. Also in 2000, new Legislative Assembly elections were held, and the sixty-six seats divided among several local and national parties.

Nezahualcóyotl (Neza) and Chalco are municipalities with their own mayors and offices, though they are still part of metropolitan Mexico City.

Mexico City is run from offices on the south side of the Zócalo. One office

building was built in the 1940s, but the other is much older. In 1527 it was the original home of the city's council.

▲ *A demonstration by members of the PRD [Partida de la Revolución Democrática], the political party founded by Cuauhtémoc Cárdenas in 1988.*

The Presidential Palace

On the east side of the Zócalo stands the National Palace, the working office of the president of Mexico. Police stand guard outside and inside the doors. When Cortés arrived almost five centuries ago, he found the Palace of Moctezuma on this spot, though the Spanish later destroyed it. The National Palace has been altered many times and parts are open to visitors. Murals painted between 1941 and 1942 by Diego Rivera, depicting the history of Mexico, grace the walls of one of the corridors. There are eleven panels that detail such scenes as the great Aztec *tianguis*, or market, in Tlatelolco.

▼ *The National Palace, remodeled in 1920, houses the president's working office. It stands on the eastern side of the Zócalo.*

Independence Day

Every September 16, Independence Day is celebrated in Mexico City. The president stands on a balcony of the National Palace to give the "Grito de Dolores," the Shout (or Proclamation) of Dolores, to crowds in the Zócalo. The proclamation dates back to 1810 when Miguel Hidalgo, a priest, first called for independence from Spain. In his village of Dolores (which was later renamed Dolores Hidalgo in his honor), located roughly 160 mi (260 km) northwest of Mexico City, Hidalgo freed prisoners, called villagers to pray, and urged them to fight the Spanish government. Today, in the Zócalo, the crowd roars their response: "Viva Mexico," or "Long live Mexico."

CHAPTER 5

Mexico City at Play

Evidence of Mexico City's cultural life is everywhere. A journey south along Insurgentes takes you past the Polyforum, designed by muralist David Alfaro Siqueiros. The unique twelve-sided building holds theaters and exhibits. The outside is painted with murals by Siqueiros. Farther on, the Insurgentes Theater is decorated with a huge mosaic by Diego Rivera, called the "History of the Mexican Theater."

The Muralists

Mexican mural art is famous worldwide. Artists used the sides of buildings, interior walls, and ceilings for gigantic paintings. The three great muralists were Diego Rivera (1886–1957), David Alfaro Siqueiros (1896–1974), and José Clemente Orozco (1883–1949). Others included Juan O'Gorman (1905–1982), who was responsible for the great mural of the "History of Mexican Culture" on the UNAM Library building. The mural movement in Mexico began in the 1920s, and many of the themes of the muralists related to the Mexican Revolution and the history of Mexico. Their work can be seen in many parts of Mexico City.

◀ Part of a mural painting in Chapultepec Castle titled the "Altar of Independence," painted by Juan O'Gorman.

A block or two away in Coyoacán is the home, now converted into a museum, that Rivera shared with artist Frida Kahlo. It is always busy as Kahlo has become a world cult figure. The studio she shared with Diego Rivera in nearby San Ángel serves as a small museum, as well.

Many exhibits of fine art, with a focus on the revolution and its followers, can be seen at the Palacio de Bellas Artes. The palace also stages classical music, opera, and dance performances, and has a Museum of Architecture on the top floor.

Music in the Open

A few blocks to the north of the Palacio de Bellas Artes is Plaza Garibaldi. On weekends, Mexico City residents and visitors gather in the plaza to listen to the sound of old Mexico. Dressed in *sombreros* (huge Mexican hats), tight black pants, and vests with silver decorations, mariachi bands play three or four violins, three trumpets, and three guitars. The name *mariachi* (from the French word for marriage) comes from the era of Emperor Maximilian when

◄ *The Palacio de Bellas Artes exhibits some of the most well-known artistic works in Mexico.*

it was traditional to hire musical groups for weddings and other fiestas.

Sporting Life

Like most Latin American countries, Mexico's favorite sport is *fútbol* (soccer). The most important games are played in the Aztec Stadium, which can seat about 114,000 spectators. The World Cup Finals have been played there twice. It is the home stadium of Mexico City's most successful team, Las Águilas. Other leading teams are the Cruz Azul and Las Pumas (the National Autonomous University of Mexico's team). The soccer season lasts from August to May and matches are like carnivals. Supporters dress up and paint their faces in their club's colors. Entire families take part and there is music and dancing. It is a great chance to see the great flowing movement of a proper "Mexican Wave" in action.

▼ *Jubilant soccer supporters gather in the Zócalo to celebrate a win by the national team.*

▲ *The bullring or "Plaza Mexico" is supposedly the largest in the world, and can seat 60,000 people.*

Bullfights

Mexico City's bullring, Plaza Mexico, is said to be the largest in the world. Bullfights are held mostly in the winter season. The drama begins at 4.00 P.M. with the sound of a trumpet, and the first of six bulls is brought into the ring. Traditionally dressed *picadors*, horse-mounted bullfighters, circle on their heavily padded horses and spear the bull. Then, the *matador*, the principal bullfighter, takes charge to kill the bull with a thrust of his sword. If the bull is killed instantly, the crowd roars approval, but if the process is drawn out, the matador is jeered.

Lucha Libre, quite simply "free fight," is one of the most popular sports in the city. It is no-rules wrestling with some local variations. The heroes of the ring give themselves fanciful names such as "Dante's Angel," and "Aztec." They wear close-fitting masks to conceal their identities. The most famous wrestler was *El Santo*—the Saint—Rodolfo Guzmán Huerta, who fought over 15,000 contests and was famous for starring in more than fifty movies.

Jai alai, said to be the world's fastest game, is another popular sport. Players hurl a ball against a wall so it bounces back with such speed that the opposition cannot catch it. They use a large, curved scoop or basket to catch and throw a ball made of rubber and goatskin. Points are scored according to where and how the ball bounces.

The Great Outdoors

In a crowded city, open spaces are a precious resource. On Sundays, many city

39

families head for Chapultepec Park, the biggest park in the city. Full of trees, lakes, and fountains, the park also holds the world-famous National Museum of Anthropology. Chapultepec Castle, the home of Mexico's president until 1939, graces one corner of the park.

Another popular site in Chapultepec Park is the children's museum, popularly known as *El Papalote*, meaning "the kite." It is filled with toys and games, a small railroad, and parts of old airplanes. Outside, there is a statue of "Cantinflas," the stage name of the famous Mexican actor and comedian, Mario Moreno Reyes.

Alameda Central is a much smaller park, but many people go there to stroll or buy a meal from the one of the many food stalls. On weekends, artists of all kinds set up their canvases and sculptures there.

San Ángel

The old village of San Ángel in the southern part of the city is a favorite place for relaxing and browsing around the Sunday markets. At one time, San Ángel was connected to the city's center by streetcars, but this was discontinued when people started using their cars or the metro more. Many grand houses remain along its cobbled streets. On Saturdays, the famous craft market known as the Bazaar Sábado is held there. The main square is filled with jewelry, pottery, leather, and clothing, and dozens of artists exhibit their work. Many tourists and middle-class Mexicans visit San Ángel to admire the paintings and handicrafts before enjoying a meal.

Xochimilco

The canals and gardens of Xochimilco are on the southern outskirts of Mexico City, about 15 mi (25 km) from the Zócalo. This is "the place where the flowers grow" on the old chinampas of Aztec times, and a large flower market is held there. Most people visit on weekends and take a boat ride through the canals. For parties, people enjoy food and music while floating down the canals on the chinampas' flat-bottomed

National Museum of Anthropology

In front of the famous National Museum of Anthropology, at the edge of Chapultepec Park, visitors are greeted by an enormous carved stone statue of the rain god Tláloc. The museum's massive, mushroom-like roof, supported by a single column, shades the main patio. Water rains down constantly, cooling passersby with a refreshing mist in the heat of summer.

wooden boats, decked with flowers. Xochimilco is one of the few places where water from Lake Texcoco still exists.

▼ *Colorful boats take visitors on a tour of the canals of Xochimilco, a favorite spot for a day out.*

CHAPTER 6

Looking Forward

Although beset by problems such as pollution, unemployment, and high crime rates, Mexico City is working hard to improve conditions. Population growth has slowed, mainly due to a changing economy. Daily life, however, is a constant challenge for everyone: for the desperately poor who have to scavenge, rob, or sell junk; and even for those better off, who still work long hours or face long journeys to work.

The elected mayor—or more correctly, the head of government for the Federal District—Andres Manuel Lopez Obrador, seems committed to revitalizing the historic center, which is a United Nations Educational, Scientific, and Cultural Organization (UNESCO) World Heritage Site. Cleaning and restoring buildings and improving safety for tourists are among the objectives. New York City's Rudolph Giuliani has been hired as a consultant to help in reducing Mexico City's high rates of kidnappings, murders, and robberies.

Rich and Poor

Few of Mexico City's economic changes have had an impact on the poorer classes. While wealthy Mexicans can afford to pay tens of thousands of dollars for a car, the minimum wage for Mexico City workers in 2002 was just $4.50 per day.

◄ *At dusk, the smog often lifts slightly and the city lights can be seen stretching past the Monument to the Revolution and on to the mountain-rimmed horizon.*

▲ *The evening crowd crosses the Avenida Lázaro Cárdenas near the Palacio de Bellas Artes.*

Housing Progress

In October 2002, the mayor opened a small housing project of 192 homes for poor families. The administration believes that since 1986—the year after the earthquake—not enough money has gone into housing. Money is now being diverted into housing projects and aid for poorer people. By the end of 2002, contributions had been made for the construction or improvement of over 40,000 housing units—part of a program to provide 60,000 new housing units every two years. In addition, 320,000 adults have been given welfare vouchers to receive basic goods; 55,000 grants have been made to people with disabilities; and 29,000 grants have been awarded to children and single mothers.

Keeping the City Moving

The government is hoping to improve transportation with extensions to main roads and viaducts. In mid-2002, the city bus transportation system had fifty-one buses specially adapted with hydraulic platforms for wheelchair passengers.

Payment for improvements to the city's infrastructure will be worth the cost in the long run. Many thousands of tourists visit Mexico City every year and account for a great part of the country's income. Investing in facilities that meet their needs will ensure that those tourists keep coming back.

Already, Mexico City's museums and galleries rank among the finest in the world, and almost everyone has tried Mexican food—it is incredibly varied and internationally famous. For these reasons, as much as for its unique culture and sheer size, Mexico City deserves its status as one of the greatest cities of the world.

Time Line

1325 Aztecs reach Valley of Mexico and found Tenochtitlán.

1473 Aztecs seize Tlatelolco.

1519 Spanish conquerors arrive in Mexico.

1521 Spaniards defeat Aztecs and occupy Tenochtitlán.

1524 First Templo de Santiago built (rebuilt 1609).

1551 The National Autonomous University of Mexico (UNAM) is founded.

1592 Alameda Central created.

1607 Work begun on draining Lake Texcoco.

1813 Metropolitan Cathedral completed.

1821 Mexico becomes a republic.

1847 U.S. attack on Mexico City.

1857–1861 New liberal government closes religious institutions, leading to civil war. The government eventually wins.

1861–62 and **1867–72** Benito Juárez president.

1864–1867 Emperor Maximilian I governs Mexico.

1864 Maximilian creates Paseo del Emperador, later known as the Paseo de la Reforma, or just the Reforma.

1876–1911 Porfirio Díaz is president.

1900 Mexico City's population reaches about four hundred thousand.

1910–1920 Mexican Revolution.

1913 Francisco Madero is assassinated.

1917 Mexico adopts a new constitution.

1939 Chapultepec Castle becomes a national monument.

1950s Mexico City's population reaches over three million.

1956 Latin American Tower built.

1962–64 Tlatelolco housing project created.

1968 Mexico City hosts the Olympic Games. Student protests end in violence.

1969 Metro opened with sixteen stations.

1976 New Basilica of Guadalupe built.

1978 Ruins of Templo Mayor discovered.

1985 Major earthquake on September 19 kills at least 10,000 and leaves 50,000 injured.

1994 Demonstrations in the Zócalo signal resistance to PRI rule, resulting in an eventual change in governing party.

1997 First mayor of Mexico City elected.

1998 Forest fires and high pollution levels force schools and factories to close.

2000 Mexico City's population reaches 8.6 million.

2002 In September, 350,000 cars are banned for a day as ozone pollution reaches dangerous levels.

Glossary

adventurers people who take part in risky ventures, often for financial gain.

aqueduct a large channel built to carry water from one place to another.

archaeologist a person who studies the remains of the world's early human history.

Art Deco a design style popular in the 1920s and 1930s featuring geometric, zigzag designs and bright metallic surfaces.

causeway way or route raised above the level of wet ground or water.

dictator a person, usually the head or ruler of a country, who governs completely and often oppressively.

flagship a ship bearing a commander's flag; or in business, the top store or product.

infrastructure the basic framework of a country, state, or region's sytem, including the resources (such as materials and personnel) it takes to perform public works.

Inquisition starting in the Middle Ages in Europe, the Inquisition was a movement for the discovery and suppression of heresy (beliefs at odds with established church teachings) within Catholicism.

maize American Indian corn.

mammoth a large, elephant-sized mammal that inhabited parts of the Earth from about three million to ten thousand years ago.

municipality an area of a town or city with local self-government.

mural a work of art painted onto (and often mixed with surfacing material to become part of) a wall or ceiling.

pilgrimage usually a journey made for a religious purpose such as visiting a holy place.

pyramid a structure usually of stone with a square base and triangular sides that meet at a single point.

rebellion citizen resistance (sometimes armed) to the ruler or government of a country.

Richter scale a scale that measures the magnitude of earthquakes.

street grid a network of streets and avenues crossing at 90-degree angles.

viaduct a long roadway elevated above the ground and supported by arches or columns.

World Health Organization the United Nations' agency for health, founded in 1948.

World Heritage Site a place or building of world importance, listed by the United Nations Educational, Scientific, and Cultural Organization (UNESCO) in Paris.

Further Information

Books

Crompton, Samuel Willard. *Tenochtitlán (Battles that Changed the World)*. Chelsea House Publishers, 2002.

Cory, Steve. *Daily Life in Ancient and Modern Mexico City (Cities Through Time)*. Runestone Press, 1999.

Linares, Fernando Orozco. *La Conquista de Mexico/Conquest of Mexico*. Panorama, 1998.

Rees, Rosemary. *The Aztecs (Understanding People in the Past)*. Heineman Library, 1999.

Steele, Philip. *The Aztec News*. Candlewick Press, 2000.

Stein, R. Conrad. *Mexico (Enchantment of the World, Second Series)*. Children's Press, 1998.

Stout, Mary. *Aztec (Native American Peoples)*. Gareth Stevens, 2003.

Web Sites

www.mexicocity.com.mx/mexcity.html
A guide to events, attractions and the city's history.

http://lanic.utexas.edu
The Latin American Information Center [LANIC] at the University of Texas at Austin.

http://www.geographia.com/mexico/mexico city/index.htm
Interesting facts and the history of Mexico City from Geographia.

http://www.tourbymexico.com/df/df.htm
This site offers general information about the Federal District and other regions of the city.

www.travelforkids.com/Funtodo/Mexico/mexicocity.htm
Outlines fun things to do when visiting the city.

www.lonelyplanet.com/destinations/north_america/mexico_city/
A comprehensive guide to the history and sights of Mexico City.

http://www.elbalero.gob.mx/index_kids.html
A kid's site about Mexico City run by the president of the Republic of Mexico.

Index

Page numbers in **bold** indicate pictures.